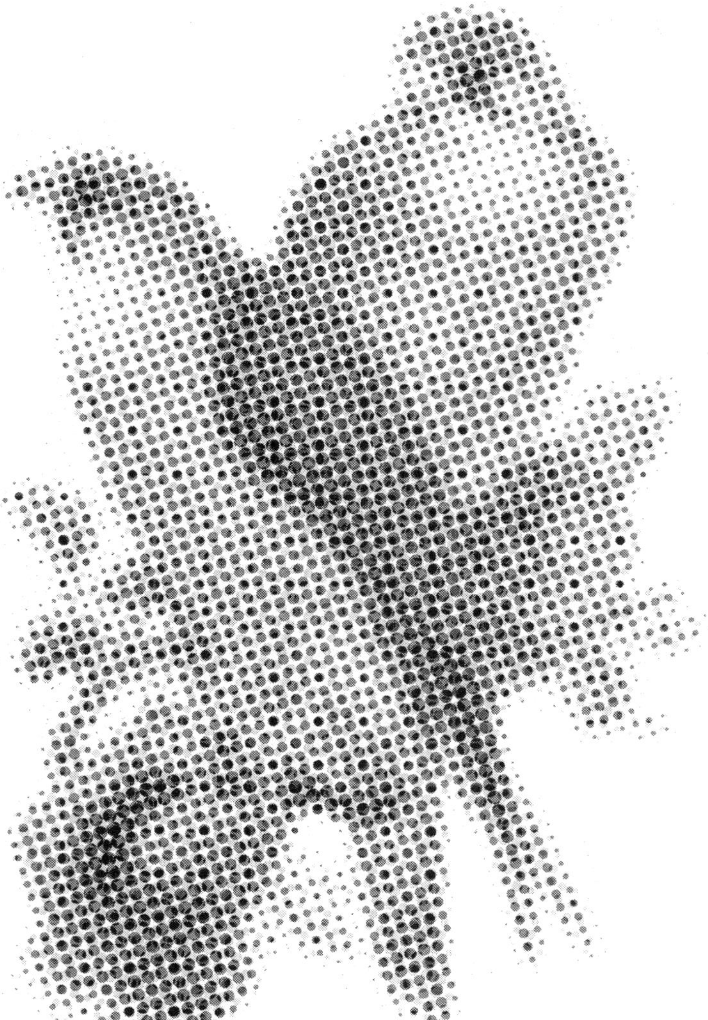

PEREGRINE

POEMS BY PAUL SOUPISET

Here, roughly at mid-life, I began writing poetry.
Actually, the poetry just started coming out:
I had intended to keep a daily journal amidst a season of life
full of transition, sadness, disappointment and misunderstanding.
But each time I sat to write, all the words came out in verse.

So be it.

I've captured this fledgling season of poetry here —
largely first drafts and fragments,
presented in no particular order. Enjoy.

Paul Soupiset, August, 2014

I AM THANKFUL FOR SEVERAL SUPPORTIVE COMMUNITIES THAT
FOSTER THE NASCENT WORK OF POETS, ARTISTS, AND WRITERS:
LAITY LODGE, THE POETRY CABAL DIASPORA, AND POETHAVEN.

PEREGRINE IS DEDICATED TO EVERYONE WHO JOURNEYED
WITH ME DURING THIS SEASON. YOU EACH KNOW WHO YOU ARE.

Moorish geometric patterns
from infidel lands
create this Christian scrim
dividing you and me
here in this
polished wooden box,
not the last I'll inhabit

for leaves and root
from brown and green
this non-machine
no stacks or soot
but trodden traipse
past apse and nave
past architrave
and wild landscapes
to woods and wild
and solitaire
no brackish air
just breath, and mild.

Vitrine peaks
and valleys formed
a perfect atoll
after the bottle cap
belied my stress.

Darker pools
have hosted worse:
nuclear lagoons.
Before Nagasaki,
Pikinni raged.

Glassy shards,
a bloody cut,
both harbingers of
my inability
to chart safe paths.

tight-knit circles
forever keep me at bay:
outside looking in.

sun-drenched patio lunch,
tacos y margaritas,
though eaten alone

2 JULY 2014 : UMBILICAL

I haven't seen
the movie about
the astronaut
becoming untethered
and floating out
into empty space.

it's bound to be
a frightening feeling,
being left alone
unto oneself with
just one's clothes,
one's inability,
one's fears
and
dwindling oxygen.

10 JULY 2014 : PICK & CHOOSE

somewhere 'tween
the morning blues
and evening news
I lost my muse;
I blew a fuse:
outside, crews
are standing 'round
instead of working
to restore power

take the tarmac
and roll it up
like fruit leather
however you see fit

make the fencepost
a shout for help
in stormweather
however you see fit

slake the drymouth
I'll cup my hands
kneebent forever
however you see fit

stake pine daggers
to flag the line
hatchet as hammer
however you see fit

break my foothold
and trip me up
I'll drink this cup
however you see fit

bake it quick or
sear it slowly, still
parallel lines run
however you see fit

prejudice and pride
Darcy's perplexed
I'll say I'm vexed
however you see fit

02 JULY 2014 : CLOCK ON THE WALL

doctors' waiting rooms
and other liminal spaces
like the times after you
open your heart and mouth
at the same time and
truth comes out but you
don't know who heard it
or how it was heard
or whether to trust
these between-places
these vestibules and
velvet-roped cueing lines
and hospice bedsides and
long drives home from pain,
these are never *los lugares*
queridas, they are never the
sought after places, but
they are the spaces where we
wait for healing, rooms with
magazine racks and mirrors
where we straighten our collars and
give our lonely selves the pep-talk
that no one can give us but God —
and we straighten our hair
and we inhale deeply when
the attendant says, "next."

31 MAY 2014 : QUICK SKETCH, SATURDAY AM

pancakes and syrup,
bacon and eggs,
coffee and cream,
dad and daughters
listening and talking

dreams unbidden arrive,
the kind that wake you
in the middle of the night;
you weigh the present now
against the shadow-world,
and negotiate a return ticket
by turning over and hoping
to return to the same spot,
the same senses, the same
half light, free from the anxiety,
free from depression, lost
in the soft folds of the tapestry

I counted every winding step,
whistled back every bird-song
that the mockingbird called down
from atop the telephone pole,
pulled weeds until I grew dizzy
from standing and stooping
and standing and stooping;
thought I could paint the
portrait or write the chorus
or hem the garment or
stir the broth the right way;
I listened to the train-whistle,
my old companion on this
Jersusalem-journey. Alone—
lonesome for David's City, perhaps.

chasing, blowing, collecting
speed and ice-crystals in
the upper atmosphere,
summoning new stormclouds
and harnessed sun-shafts,
the spirit flew east
and hovered over
one small boy's hut.
squinting into the
night-made-day,
the boy held tightly onto the
white door-casing,
but the spirit passed over him
and reversed course, blowing
west-by-northwest
until, past conifer and juniper,
the spirit hovered over
a sickly girl's *tipee*.
instead of glowing like
the noonday sun, the
spirit rang like silvery bells.
through the animal skins
the girl shook, not with fever,
but retreating fear,
and so the spirit passed over her also,
and changed directions.
Moments later and halfway
across the planetary arc,
the spirit enveloped a
sleeping stowaway, lifting
her out of her hiding place
below the decks of the sailing vessel
and depositing her safely
into a childless woman's arms,
thousands of leagues away
near a fire-pit.

"I said, 'Father, change my name.'"
— LEONARD COHEN

Once-deaf,
I leaned in
and traded
my name back again.
No longer Paul,
no longer *small*.
The once-blind and
goad-kicking Saul
saw paradise: *Sol*, sun,
Kerouac's Sal Paradise, or
McCarthy's ashen son's bivouac.
The once-dumb ask us
"Who wants Damascus?"
100 Straight Street or
The Haight-Ashbury Street
diner where Joanne smiled.
Give up my name, any fame,
this game, now lame duck,
I wait.

antebellum
before coming to blows

antediluvian
before coming rainbows

cerebellum
all in my head

the drain
(the chrome thing
at the bottom of
the drain).

the stopper,
connecting
to the bottom by
a chain.

the porcelain
is chipping
at the bottom, and
is stained.

the claw-feet,
upholding
the tub-bottom,
a gryphon,

a siphon:
downspouting,
draining the bottom, a
rain-tornado.

a cypher,
I'm waiting,
sitting on my bottom in
an empty tub.

I.
Upon a king's mountain,
I had scrawled a poem
without rhyme or meter
or much thought,
contouring out the
mastodon in the drawing-room,
and reciting as I composed,
because who wants their
friends to be trampled,
who wants themselves to
be crushed
tied and tethered by Yeats'
monstrous thing:
trapped within scraps
of paper, close
to the fireplace, close to the
lectern, and in full view of
the poet's judging ones.
All I had un-rhymed,
was it hesychasm?
Or masochism?
Let's move inside and
keep talking.

II.
Lowering myself
into dry wells that echo my
calls for drink, for Olympic
lanes in which to tread,
oceans in which to drown,
icewater pints to down.
Pozo Seco sings again but
this, too is dust: dead birds,
carpenters and ladies.

Yeats again, parlor-mammoths
and women laughing;
packed trunks and hasty maps,
hastier naps, and fear and
sandy sea-bottoms with
the pressure of the submariner,
the clarity of saltwater eyes,
an oxygen line that disappears
up toward the surface.

III.
My son, let the elephant stay,
unannounced. Even if he violently
sweeps your house with his
tail; all animals have stories to tell.
He may be clearing you
out of house and home;
sucking the air
out of the room, but do not
point him out to friends.
Perhaps they are terrified
of the gray or the fray;
let it stay; let them stay.
They are human, too.
They feel deeply too.
Their grays are not
your grays, just as
God's thoughts are
higher than our thoughts.

(Prone to wander, prone to leave.)

---

26 JUNE 2014 : AN APPROPRIATED BLESSING

"Peace to your chaos. Somehow."

---

25 JUNE 2014 : PROTESTANT, TO MARY, MOTHER OF GOD

Mother Mary,
What do you see?
How much, beyond the veil?
Is the scrim less opaque?
Do you pray for us?
Meddle?
Protect us from mishap?
What of *rapprochement*?
What news of unity?
Does Francis dance with David?
Do Moses and Enoch talk much?
Moreover,
Will my heart be made whole?
Does bread still smell as sweet?

---

25 JUNE 2014 : SMELLS

concentrated eucalyptus
oxidized patchouli

baseball glove conditioning salve
steel-tin three-in-one gun oil

pillows that smell like you
morning coffee, morning bacon

we smell our way to heaven

---

we struggle we learn we are met with affliction we build bonfires to push back the now we sew fig leaves to cover our naïveté we sing lullabies to sooth our inner one we fingerpaint cloudy masterpieces we unbend marshmallow coat hangers we listen to grasshoppers

---

24 JUNE 2014 : FRAME

I.
curbside picture frame
empty inside, gilt edges,
so I took it home

II.
appropriated
(grabbed by my oldest daughter).
back to framelessness.

---

24 JUNE 2014 : NO STARCH, PLEASE

spreadsheets,
timesheets,
bedsheets
all make me
feel the same.

give me a blank
sheet of paper
and I'm at home
in my skin.

the depression was bad
the anxiety is worse
but the lack of sleep
is the real demon
crippling in so many ways
insomnia creates dry husks
from well-intentioned
tender hearts
makes us react in off ways
makes our reaction times slower
makes us reactionary
hands out involuntary facial tics where there
were none, and other muscle spasms;
these movements ripple
out into the world
unintentionally
hurting others in the process.
today's three-hour nap
felt great, but I'll need another tomorrow, and come Monday
I'll need one but have no way to take one.
if God is kind and hands restful sleep back to me at some point, if my
fears are allayed, and if my shadow season can recede, if I stop replaying
and start forgiving myself, I might feel like me again.

I have prayed for you, sir,
every day since March.
You barely know me, yet you
think you know me.

---

clearing
the tallus and tailings
like the hike to the punchbowls
uphill from the Glen

bouldering
the larger ones
like the hike at Hackberry's creek
or the climb up Enchanted Rock.

but this place also is a clearing
nonified with a determiner,
not just a gerund, but a
person place or thing.

---

sometimes
my heart is
emptied out
unto fullness.

sometimes
I take and grab
and hold on
unto emptiness.

waxed paper,
confectioners' sugar

I. MON AMI, CHARLEROI

crowns and crayons
songs, forgotten songs.
the etymology of *chandeliers*
blinders and beeswax,
a fuse and a wick and a
spark and a stick
and a coyote and a chaparral.
your Belgian home before we met
(but that was decades ago).

II. MÉTHODE CHAMPENOISE

chants and chancel-rails,
moths, mopping-pails.
the face in the bathroom mirror
heroine and horror,
fermented in a cave,
uncorked with a wave
and a wink and a nod.
my appellation is perhaps Acadian
(though neither Appalachian nor a Cajun).

III. CHAPERONED CHARCUTERIE

pork *rillettes* and citrus terrine,
Dublin® sodas, time with my son.
the ecclesiology of tables shared
comforting and sobering,
we walk the same lawn
we're here then we're gone;
a semester and a trimester.
may you return to the nest when needed
(nest-egg notwithstanding).

26 MAY 2014 : CURVILINEAR

the thick-thin arc
of the watercolor stroke
traces contours
observant eyes have recorded;
first wet, then color-loaded,
a beautiful bleeding,
inhabiting space:
incarnation in
peaches, blush,
browns, blue,
pale reds, bronze,
sparse charcoal and
saintly gold.

23 JUNE 2014 : SKIN & BONES

black feather
white feather
limestone and dirt

I turned around to see
diaphanous gauze
asynchronously

daylight
midnight
concentric waves

I turned again to see
Sellenger's Round
with passing pilgrims

a burdening
a bird-wing of driftwood
a burgeoning ship of fools

I turned again to tromp over
weeds and avoid flowers
sweat-beads forming

Trompe-l'œil
I swore you were there,
skin and bones

crown of thorns
white feather
my brother

poet, priest, prophet, king
Kyrie Eleison
between alliance and dalliance

Nail-scarred hands
the weight of the world
on those shoulders

See? I make all things new.

+

---

12 MAY 2014 : SATURDAY

daydreaming in bed;
high thread count sheets hasten my
procrastination

No motorists this evening.
The light spills out from solitude
and Wilson works the gas-pump row:
the oil and gas, supposed to save
this little burg from poverty.

The gasoline is primed to flow
but Cadillacs and Plymouths go
the northern route, and duty calls
our man to stay and man his post

While wingéd Pegasus reminds,
or mocks, at least, "*Stabilitas.*"
The pilgrimage, the far-off hill,
the empty road, this trinity:
combustible, convertible, insatiable.

The Franchise Man will visit soon
to see how Wilson's station fares.
He doesn't make it out here much,
so, disenfranchised, Wilson stands.

(*upon viewing* GAS, *1940, by Edward Hopper*)

I scaled the
infinite ladder
— squintingly tall —
and it (leaning
against what I did
not know), held fast.
so up I went.

My son, eat this bread,
broken for you.
My daughters, drink deep,
and thirst no more.
My beloved, take off your sandals;
for this is holy ground.
Shall I stay silent?
Can gravel cry out?
Bread. Eat. Cup. Pass.
But not my will.

I was doing quite well, thank you.
This camouflage God's gift
Rent and rendered torn asunder
Oriflamme standard bearer
Impales torchbearer inflames arms-bearer
punching at the wind, punching at the wind, punching at the wind.

the word
the symbol
the sign and signified
sharpening pencils
staring at quatrefoils
for hours at a time,
days upon nights upon days,
standing within fora,
praying that
I would hit the mark
not miss the mark
create a mark
erasures, connected lines,
solitude, silence,
abandonment,
four-leafed clover,
make a
mark, fourfold
matthew, mark,
luke, john at or near
threshold's curvilinear benches,
come sit with me
teach me some enlightenment
guide my hand
eagle, lion, ox, man,
sun and moon and stars
while my heart cries out
for four
and my home moves from
six to five
and my godhead is three, is one
and my wounds come in twos
and I stand or sit as one
lonely figure

my death-shadow
hasn't yet caught up
with my skin;
it is trailing
at a safe distance,
my only desert companion.
sandy, solitary,
a lone follower
following a lone walker,
he at half opacity:
multiplied and
gaussian-blurred,
but offset.

he looks like me,
smells like acrid breath,
and doesn't bother
with niceties.
I walk or crawl
in circular ruts
scribed by the
outer highway loop
of the last American city.

he plays along and
apes my halting movements.
perhaps he is meant to be
my friend in this wilderness,
whip-stitched onto my corpus
with needle and floss,
so at least he cannot bail.

"You're with me, Sombra.
 Rest unseen under
 the loquat tree."

staying hidden for a season,
camouflage-gift, mosaic quail,
backroads taken with good reason.
avoiding pale makes a paler pale,
ruddy, blushing,
bloody, rushing,
draining the pink from my waning face and hearing my pulse in my
waxing ears and shaking, the shaking hands and legs
surprised me.
less than some edenic fruit,
an alternating driving route,
hide me, angels, in your feathers
until my coal-touched lips
can form the words
until my brimstone eyes
can look unflinchingly
at the face of what?
forgiveness? anger?
vengeance? another
set of camouflage?
wisdom? rage? a change?
a turned page, a *peace-out.*

Huevos, frutas, ovarios,
Nidos y verdes jardines, éstos
En su tiempo señalado
serán participantes en su trabajo

1. HAIKU AT THE CATTLE GATE

fences and fencing
(like pickets and picketing)
should not be confused.

2. HAIKU AT THE GOLDEN GATE

santo francisco
dancing naked with the birds
like a golden bridge

3. HAIKU FOR MY FRIEND NAMED GATE

audio signals
often pass through a threshold
(it's called a noise gate).

4. HAIKU AT WHITEFRIARGATE

micklegate in york?
a passageway called a bar;
hell's gate is not barred

5. HAIKU AT THE PEARLY GATE

new yorker cartoons
show st. peter at the gate
(a chili's® hostess).

6. HAIKU FOR A LIMPING GAIT

soft, the sunrise spies
my homeless friend on concrete:
sot, sleeping, childlike.

7. HAIKU FOR THE GATOR

refrigerator's
floridian orangeade
(i'll see you later)

8. HAIKU AT THE GARDEN GATE

a friendship hinges
upon a six-by-six post,
steady as she goes

9. HAIKU AT THE CITY GATE

come, let us reason
—sojourners, philosophers—
in afternoon shade

10. HAIKU AT THE CEMETERY GATE

let them all fall down
these scraps of ephemera
belong in the ground

XII.
The last shall be first.

I.
A Fredericksburg farm,
A graduation day,
A *matryoshka* factory,
A Seattle hospital room,
A faceless imaging lab,
A labor & delivery room,
A makeshift confession booth.
(My twin. Birds. Eggs. Beauty.)

II.
When we were still inside the womb
A shackled, fearful symmetry,
Like Esau's odd fraternity with
Grasping Jacob's epitaph
Our frames were hidden not from God,
Though frames without a photograph.

III.
We all like Russian nesting dolls
Or layers of an onion-skin
Are blind to who we once had been
And ever-bearing what befalls:
The brave Salutatorian,
the would-be mother, nursing wounds

IV.
And near the Whitworth's Orchard loam
They watch and wait for ripening
These tiny buds that blossom unto
Pitted peach and nectarine

To walk again among the rows
Of shady trees; to pluck and pull and
Place them into cardboard boxes,
Bushel-halves of mid-July.

VII.
Brother hawk and sister robin,
Aviary, nesting, free
Calling out like *Jean-Baptiste,*

"Level then the path ahead,
Once-serpentine, now straighten, ye!"

VIII.
Nests are empty oftentimes,
Their baby birds have flown away
To test their own wet wings amidst
The burning noonday helium

These twigs and stems encircling
The orbed impression of an egg

IX.

(Some have fallen prey or
fallen down or fallen short)

Ovoid ripened bird-like dreams,
Horse hairs
Woven prayers into the
Hollow saddle of her nest
Avoiding talk of stirrups
    or bridles

(Eggs and fruit and ovaries,
Nests and verdant gardens, these
Will in their own appointed time
Be players in your work sublime)

X.

The photograph, the CT scan,
The darkroom and the aperture
Belie the beauty deep within.
Exposure's harsh, but harsher still
The liminal entablature
That presses down and presses in

XI.

Brother, Mother, Sister, Friend,
Blood-kin, In-Law, Married-In,
Sinner, Saint, Confessor; God

(Breathe, child. Say what you mean.)

a stake in the ground
a chance for your younger self
to breathe in kindness

what was once the barren side-yard tree
whose sloughed-off branches bothered me last June
surprised me as I walked around the back:
a starch-white burning bush, and none too soon.

like millefleur on Flemish tapestries
it called me closer, squinting as I walked,
as I approached, each flower, sharply seen
full-burst to life, despite this once-dead stock

but, juxtaposed with Clotho, Atropos,
or measuring Lachesis, weft and warp'd
no weaver's hand, and no *Triumph of Death*
but life's triumphant blossoms I absorbed.

And every flower had its tending bee;
The whole scene caught me, taken unawares.
The branches, come to life, were humming, free,
A god-wrought thing that flickers as it flares

The gift of noticing was happenstance.
A mundane trash-can run was what surprised.
I'd still just think it only kindling-wood
If I had never opened up my eyes.

The Swede keeps dogs;
the Dane drinks tea.
The house was white
originally.
But sparked a fire
By stricken matches
well before
the fireman's badges
turned away
from charcoal halls,
and writing off
these blackened walls,
the color of the house
was this,
—if only in
the interstice—
A cardinal hue
you'd not forget,
burning, *House
of Capulet.*
the Brit remembered
only red,
although the whitewash'd walls
had led him
once to praise its purity —
its embers must have
addled thee.

what bright lunations: solar rays,
these aureoles from M-16s
or Gatling guns on gilded days
past Orioles, the passerines.

we're made of star-stuff, made of suns
these shafts and slits of glitter-dust
form spotlight arcs from loaded guns
that pierce the stratocumulus.

¿Quién no tiene miedo?
¿Dónde está la luz?
el corazón que
desea la paz,
el alma que
suspira por amor,
éstos son mis maestros,
éstos son mis
compañeros-de-peregrinación.
los Santos oran por usted.
la gran nube de los santos
ve su dolor.

¿Quién puede decir
palabras de institución?
¿Quién puede escuchar
los suspiros de Dios?
¿Quién puede reclamar
el camino superior?
¿Quién puede prevenir
el daño involuntario?
¿Dónde está la luz
de la mañana?

i

I look back on beautiful small bungalows in which we've lived:
Montclair Street, Chevy Chase Drive, Irvington.
Each standing at the more affordable periphery
Just outside the enclaves of old-monied neighborhoods.

"They're Post War Victory Homes", the buyer's agent offered
"Great starter homes", a magazine headline reported.
But this wasn't our first mortgage, and it wasn't always victory.
Hours sanding, hours painting. I hated sweat. I hated toil.
"Maintenance-free", was my unmet God-asked epithetic.

ii

Home is rootedness, presupposing venture.
I think back on the pilgrimage, the Camino,
The small sparrow who found her escape,
Flutter'd from my clumsy ribcage,
Just like Ireland's Brendan, far-traversing.

I think back on the hermitage, the Cenobite,
Old Pangur Bán, finding some warmth and rest
Underneath the drafting-table,
Saint Aiden's purring familiar.

iii

I plunged myself down into the dark, shady-green,
Barefooted through the St. Augustine,
near the live-oaked edge of Rock Creek,
Which runs dry except for rare noetic deluge-days
It ran nonetheless; it ran sacred through my back yard.
I was that boy again, and trusted and breathed, but hesitated,
Wishing my callouses were all underfoot, not guarding a heart.

I played down by the creek, up in my tree-house,
Where I learned to fight, and fear, and flee, build and break and mend.
In my kingdom, hearing my middle name uttered was
Shorthand for, "Stop. Come. Dinner's ready."
That boy walked back up to the house and shed his skin.
But he longs to be rooted, mothered, tethered and still.

iv

My father was a homebuilder.
He built us a fine home on a fine lot, played his role.
My mother was a homemaker.
She stayed and made and cultivated all manner of growing things.

water-bearer
solitary figure
pouring clay-encased
red-walled,
black-glazed
cradled hydriai.
freshwater, saltwater,
stillwater, sweetwater,
it's all salve, living,
staving off thirst.

daughter, cistern
lonesome carrier, now
filling earthen vessels
with new wine:
deep purples
ladled from the cask.
plucked, bruised,
crushed, stomped,
it's a violent mash,
fermenting for years.

broken amphora,
pierced deftly by your
well-placed bungs,
stoppers, and spigots:
each measure life out
in graduated drops.

but careless wear and tear
creates fissures
best seen when held
to the light.
droplets become
rivulets become
torrents carrying shards.

there's no need to
measure with perfect
composure the
drips from the spout
when water falls out
like violet oceans
from the back of the urn

28 MAY 2014 : (HAPPY)

do you remember
the name of the goldfish
I brought to surprise you
in the dormitory lobby

and if I bought you
the same gift, but today,
two long decades later,
I think its name would be the same

29 MAY 2014 : UTTER RUIN

Beat your breast, O prisoner.
Jerusalem lays in bloody ruins.
Who can rebuild its splendor?

I sink to the bottom as a stone.
"I desire a pure and contrite heart,"
scrawled his finger on the wall.

Pharaoh and his chariots are
cast into the foaming red sea.
The depths have devoured them.

The law is a millstone, its fulfillment
a pebble hitting a sandy bottom,
coming to rest on the ocean floor.

Perhaps the seahorse knows the Prophet;
perhaps the reef will
raise up on the last day.

29 JUNE 2014 : BOTH/AND

Saint-Étienne,
stand ever in
the middle,
holding both
coffee and tea,
marking the
via media
with your
Swiss Miss®
neutrality.

30 MAY 2014 : CHALICE & SHROUD

the barque steadies
and slips, embarks
into the infidels' river
a break in the solder-silver.
the waters still are
coming to the crew's aide
in the night,
coming to the crusade
is the knight;
their going is feudal,
their coming is futile,
thematically fugal:
In hoc signo vinces
undertaker winces
while now overtaking
Sangreal's death-drums.
Crimson crosses upon
white fields, but the inverse
is more true, ghostly, and bloodied.

it wouldn't help
to explain it all anyway.
any mental picture
that might emerge,
from wildflowered
sheep-shorn pastures
to hellbent hydroplaning,
would be off by degrees.
My story will die with me, Guildenstern offered.
They don't want
the truth anyway.
Abe is scrambling to find the ram.
Mountainous switchbacks
Where is the scapegoat
that will appease our present
conception of the divine?
The altar has been built,
Four hasty cairns and a grate,
Rosencrantz reminded.
Feign madness,
Even in your sacred words,
feign madness.
You are no spotless lamb but
the twelve tribes can use you
to bear away the darker markings.
Gilded *sturm und drang* what say you?
Then, slowly:
I'll don the foolscap knowingly
Gesture wildly, feigning incoherence
to make my point.
I'll nail my reputation to a tree
Trade my good name for a handful of magic beans
I'll work up spittle and pretend I'm rabid
I will limp around, wild-eyed with a hunchbacked gait
if debasing myself buys others their freedom.
I'm your man.

29 JUNE 2014 : TERMINAL MINOTAUR — FRAGMENT

chained to a post
in a clearing
under the
tall-treed canopy.
useless years have
passed since I last
attempted to loosen
these irons that keep me.
my mostly silent captors
long ago scribed
radiating chalk rays
running straightaway
from the center stake,
marking my line of sight
in and around the conifers.
The parts I make out
are desolate and punishing
and I wouldn't believe
the flourishing network
of beauty they've built
behind the trees, in between the
upkept powdered
lines, their arcs of life.

22 MAY 2014 : EARLY SUNDAY MORNING — AFTER HOPPER

This is my father's world
Lentils and beams, concrete and wood
The tilt-shift bygone neighborhood
stands flat, hollow.
But, mind the plate-glass
Examine the signage,
Move in closer, boy.
See these letters:
Gold-leaf serifs,
China-white sans,
Majuscule and minuscule,
A capital idea; and lo, the ampersand,
The local sign painter, my great-uncle Charles,
Preferred display type, but could be counted upon
To hand-render a help-wanted sign,
Should the barber inquire.

(upon viewing EARLY SUNDAY MORNING, *1930, by Edward Hopper)*

27 MAY 2014 : CHOICES WERE MADE

I am implicated in every tide pull
Every handshake, even
half a world away
Every dying child or slave,
Every kiss exchanged, every
signature on every letter,
Every rash or thoughtful decision
Every hard-won scrap of resolve;
His coming in, her going out,
their backchannel, their narrow,
Byzantine alleyways,
connecting enemies,
creating enemies,

offering palm branches before crucifixion and clasping
olive branches in beaks and
grasping forbidden fruit and
truffling for bidden root and node and
it's all silken webwork
and just as fragile.

---

28 MAY 2014 : ANOTHER PSALM

The lemonade
has been stirred
and the sugar
put back on its shelf
but the flat, damp rinds
remain on the countertop,
and they are me.

There's no juice
left for you to extract.
You can hoist me back
onto the machine
and turn the handle tighter
all you want,
but tartness has
turned to bitterness,

and what you think you're
extracting won't be what
your torque will yield.
better to give up now

and let me lie here in peace.

Here, the understood you.
Here, the tacitly observed object; we both know it is there.
Today, a book, unbroken spine.
Tomorrow a pen, or a matchstick,
Or a plastic cup, with ice and soda.
And you nose around until, satisfied and secure,
My space becomes your space,
The most gentle intrusion,
The most winsome of trespasses.
What you want, you get.
What you want, you take.
Your curiosity will never kill
Because you stay fickle.
My curiosity just may do me in.

fleeting.
a darkroom light leak,
exposing more than paper,
a lingering teenage buss,
the ghostly veil
of old young joy,
chasing daylight,
belaying trust off
a low-tide castle,
your glance,
your shoulders,
like
pinhole
photography,
fleeting.

(with stylistic apologies to Edgar)

Looking out the church-door peep-hole
In the shadow of the steeple
I can see we've dug a deep hole
In the cemetery yard

So aerial, these white-washed spires;
Funereal, your flaming pyres;
The burial of our desires
In the cemetery yard

Dirt dug straight and fresh and squared-off
Tall pall-bearers matched and paired off:
Members here, so they're not scared off
By the cemetery yard

The AM radio conspires,
Its gospel-hour hymn inspires
They couldn't pay for proper choirs
In the cemetery yard

The service started on the hour
Brassy bells tolled from the tower
I watched it all beneath the bower
By the cemetery yard

Your exit strategy was grand
Yet more dramatic than you planned
I wish I could give you a hand
Out of the cemetery yard

You're given unto your release
The narrative can finally cease
But I don't think you'll rest in peace.
+

coffee-ring circles
crescent moons on the napkin
signify morning

"Watch your step."
The brilliant white corridor
bisected with the line of
charcoal colored singing tire swings
gave way to your grandmother's
ceiling-fanned mudroom,
a proper Victorian vestibule which had,
at its long-leaf pine plank center,
a newly ravaged, single narrow garden row
an ellipse splintering the floorboards, its rich soil spilling
onto the wood and perforated here and there
with sprouting silver spoons which you so lovingly
plucked and placed in the makeshift basket
formed in the folds of your floor-length skirt,
taking care to prune any intruding
shrimp forks or butter knives
that forked off from the stems.

"Let's begin."
Your composure was remarkable even after the
coat closet's ladle tree refused to yield
any of her polished, argentine fruit.
You never demurred,
spine erect, shoulders back, into the powder room as you
spun the porcelain HOT and COLD handles,
allowing its steaming tomato soup to fill the basin.
Too hot to eat.

You took my hand and we walked silently to the guest parlor,
where, above Queen Anne's legs, you uncovered
the draped grinding wheel and turned the handle and
sanded the raw spoon fingerlings until the silvery ends
were rounded and moon dust lay upon the table.

"Such noises."
In my daydream, your tears swept the streets clean,
but in reality you stood and found your uncle's walking cane
and pierced the side table with it —
first placing a wine stem beneath the borehole —
and an issuance of merlot and cabernet came forth.

"Almost."
The sitting room contained arrows and a yew-bow
and you pulled the line taut and the arrow shot
and pierced the loaf of freshly baked bread.
You closed your eyes and whispered incantations
and brought back to life the bearskin rug;
the wall-mounted deer and mouflon slowly
craned their necks to watch the feast begin.

"What gift of happiness?"
A terrarium? A bowl for a gold-fish? A pillow?
Just a skeleton key on a chain, to be worn around your neck,
as the home creaks and grows and envelopes you.

"We must not linger."
Later, we made our way through the dining room forest,
parting aspen branches, stepping over burnt conifer logs,
until we found a clearing to spread my blanket.
We ignored the door chime.
Your circlet was thorny, your dress stained red in places by the bisque.
So statuesque. You would make a terrible muse
because I would always stay distracted, never again to work.
even so, come.

the midsummer
cicada horde
drones loudly
in my ears as the
eleven o'clock heat
swelters, buzzing,
and sends sweat rivulets
from my now pounding head
trickling unimpeded
past my eyebrows
and straight into
my bloodshot eyes
already squinting
from the loosened
paint flecks and sawdust,
but I can only
squeeze my eyes tightly
and pray that the
stinging August saline
continues its
downward slide
because my left hand is
holding steadily
onto the blistering
metal ladder
while my right hand
manages a putty knife,
reaching and scraping
old wooden siding on this
whitewashed
depression-era
garage.
here and there
brittle lead-based
slivers of dried

housepaint create
bamboo shoots
under my fingernails.
I'm snowblind under this
inescapable summer sun,
dizzy upon the ladder
and now nauseated.
After hours
of grating, abrading
and debriding boards,
I'm beyond spent
but sanding will come next.
My shirt, underwear and shorts
are soaking wet by one-thirty.
My arms and shoulders
and thighs and knees
are sore and will be
worse tomorrow,
but this is nothing;
it is my craning neck and
throbbing, sunburnt forehead
and these stinging eyes
that make me resent
what seems like
forced labor.

---

22 MAY 2014 : VERANDA

Two long years had passed
since the steps were mended.
Sitting on her bed, the forgotten child
remembers some important detail.
I can't quite make out the movements of her mouth;
I am no lip reader.

were you there
when they crucified?
my LORD, were you
there when the bottle broke?
when the story was
squandered?
when the pen slipped and slid
comparing pain,
complicit rain,
completely sane,
were you?

The bread and cup, they said,
were sacrament.
Basin, towel, and pitcher
were never meant
to be elevated
to holy rite.

We, quite easily could
have selected
washing each other's feet:
so connected
to the elemental;
to terrine stuff.

Not once, but twice this week
my feet have been
baptized within these walls:
but with two ends:
to be consecrated;
to simply wash.

a fountain pen exploded.
a bleeding oxford stain.
a navy bullet wound.
a pocket, freshly ironed.
the seeping ink now wasted,
intended for a sonnet
or a travelogue or
grocery-list upon a
diner napkin or a
signature, indelible,
but now a blot to mar the shirt
that just this morning
signified a workday's start.
Should I even bother, then
to snip the threads and save
the buttons so some other
day some other cuff or collar
might be benefited?
Either way the cloth is now
a rag.

let me be found
let me be lost so that
I can be found
"God is my clearing;
this place is a clearing;
I am a clearing"
let me be lost
let me be found so that
in the finding
I can be lost again
and found again

13 APRIL 2014 : ART SUPPLIES

I opened the door to find the morning wet
and then remembered the baskets
of art supplies left out overnight.
Brushes and paint-jars would be fine,
but the posterboard sign and the
tagboard ribbon spools wouuld be ruined;
waterlogged organza, grosgrain, and satin
with sopping pink yarn-balls and the
basket handles were coming undone.
I salvaged what I could, then noticed
the dew upon the stems and branches:
clinging glassy strings, suspended
like Murano beadwork
on Fortuny's famous gown.
The art was made in spite of me.

22 JUNE 2014 : FRAGMENT FROM LATE MAY

the path of Rock Creek
when viewed from my
childhood family room
runs from left to right
down at the bottom
of our property line.

Up here is the sofa, the *Saltillo*,
the O'Neil-Ford-inspired brickwork
the glass patio doors
the barstool where I'd
sit and watch for hours
as my mother painted *batik*
and watercolor, sculpted clay
or soldered stained glass.

11 JULY 2014 : THE GIVENNESS OF CIRCLES

beneath the town, beneath.
   rubbleshake and Hubblecleared
and mumble-on with stubblebeard
   you stumblepon this tumbledown
i troublemake eat humblepie
   that rumblesky does doubletake
you doubledown eat crumblecake
   past shavenbeard and trouble-sky
a triplecrown, a thund'rous-sigh
   beneath the lake, beneath the ground.
beneath the sky, beneath.

17 APRIL 2014 : SO WE SMILE BACK

The night has arrived and we've all padded our way to the
agreed upon gathering place. A moment of silence at the
shoreline here to center ourselves. The timepiece says 11:35.
Unsure and groping, strangers and friends and confidants,
we ease the coracle away from taut tethers, free from boulder
and block, down a few feet into lapping, slapping tide.
This band of five women, three men, sit in silence as we
embark. The moon asks us no questions but only smiles.

10 MAY 2014 : HAIKU

ambient, diffuse,
the morning fog is lifting,
leaving us naked

a perseverance package
is never as golden as the
parachute; if every mile-marker
and exit sign looks the same,
if every off-ramp degrades
at the same angle of repose,
if every avoidance, every
backroad I've turned to
stay camouflaged earns
the same insouciance,
then why be like Dilsey?
Shall I continue? I shall continue.
Can I endure? How can I not?
Lie low, my friend,
keep your head down,
assume the best in people.
Endure.

my footlocker full of
cassette mix-tapes
is just sitting there,
out in the garage,
audible memories
oxidized and overrun
by silverfish.
it wouldn't take much
effort
to save most of them,
but the disappointment
in not being able
to save all of them
keeps me from
opening the lid.

15 MAY 2014 : FOUNDLING

deer-blind.
headlights.
camouflage.
his prayer has been
for camouflage
these forty days.
field-dressed,
hung,
blood-drained red.
but he asks for
swatches of brown
and patches of
sand and green;
sticks and stones,
and, then,
leaves.

12 APRIL 2014 : CLEANING MY OFFICE

sorting through
workaday
detritus
I'm no Midas
and this shinola
I've amassed
is a bit
like humus,
a soiled past,
humorous that I hold on,
that I hoard memories
the way I do.
no gold here. just
artifacts and opinions to
shakedown
and discard

revisiting a poem begun in 2008

the hour growing late,
pregnant
with this project, with possibilities,
i lifted the front edge of my
tee-shirt to form a chalky cloth sling

i piled in hands full of
fist-sized limestone
three, nine, thirty-eight,
and i labored to stand,
grabbing my back,
looking and feeling
like a last-trimester mama -
and i laughed out loud.
this father of four births,
four umbilical incisions,
four afterbirths,
and one miscarriage,
waddling over to this
birthing site,
pacing in artistic anticipation,
wondering and worrying
about this strange,
forthcoming delivery

so many strong women
in my life,
many of them mothers,
and some of them
wing-waiting

i figured they'd all
laugh out loud
(perhaps my twin-bearing
mom the loudest)
to see me wrestle and
wrangle and huff

i came around
to where i'd left off

i couldn't gracefully
set my quarry upon the earth
so i squatted
and, Valsalva,
let the stones

fall

a little lower than the angels

had the earth tonight been water
the concentric rippled labyrinth
might have serv'd witness enough

to the father, son and holy ghost.

forgive my ambertrapped
disorientation
the slow emerge
the clayfooted scansion
as my head swims through
cathedric murmurs
and underwater pings
forgive my absence:
the afternoon slipped into night.
I slept while you worked,
chauffeuring and
making dinner for the children.

---

9 MARCH 2014 : FOURTH STREET AT SAN JACINTO

i have lost my car.
i am perrfectly sober and yet
i have lost my car
in downtown austin.
every surface lot looks the same
this late at night
and i forgot to dress warmly
and what's worse i am alone.

---

10 MARCH 2014 : COMING BACK EARLY

taking shelter from
the rain
we order tomato basil soup
and chips
and sandwiches.
three of us
placed
around the bistro table.
the poet, the writer, the artist.

but we have other designs tonight.
we discuss love and loss,
similarly shaped scars,
and paths toward
some tenable future,
staving off the demons
that would do us in.
soup bowl grows cold
as conversation warms.
tonight, i am not alone.

laying low, for everyone's good.
praying now, for just a
flicker, flame or lit filament
from some squirrel-cage
edison bulb hanging in
my chest: are you there,
swinging there?

o god, this mess we made:
are you not implicated?
what is the essence,
and how connected?
it's all love, but
all's not love, and
i was supposed to be better by now.

screaming alone is one thing.
but to bring you
along for the ride —
innocent, more or less,
at least by comparison,
by degrees,
was to do violence to you.
i swerved.
you screamed.
we died. we awoke.

hydroplaning
with a child's heart
and grey in his beard
and push, pull,
abandon
abandoned
he mis-steered and veered
into the curb.
that's when you said in a panicked plea,
"let me out."
the image is seared onto his mind
that's when he turned
into a parking lot and
let you out.
he gave you his keys
and you drove him back
safely in the rain

— fin

13 MARCH 2014 : I'VE CREATED A MONSTER (EXCERPT)

"i've created a monster."
i said this about you
more than once,
in my head, smiling, proud..

i said the same words,
unmiling, unflinching, out loud.
forcing myself to
reckon my own countenance

in the mirror
at the doubletree,
just hours after parting ways,
a day after the incident.

i believed once that relationships
were my domain.

i've created paintings,
drawings, children, love, in my time.
i've created a monster,
and the monster isn't you.

cloth of death
bearing this casket
cloth of life
covering eucharistic chalice

resting in one's being
to have existed, breathing
participle, past:
your work is finished

to stir at the coals
convinced that fire will come
conjuring and inciting
hearth-gathered embers

to graze beyond the bullseye
fletching dart and point
to remain the beginner
as kind consignment

white fields' boll-and-lint
lenten bowl
for the fabric of life
easing the painful rending

pall, been, kindle, sin, and gin

revisiting a poem begun in 2004

the fire came to us
on Thanksgiving
downwind
from the house on the hill
and by the time
i saw it
the first field had burned.
we flew.
bobcats traced fire-breaks
and that girl
borrowed my camera
and the Five Points VFD
and others finally arrived.
shovels were handed out
and confident men
turned into firefighters.
and the rest of us?
— we stomped
and surveyed
the helplessness
of helplessness
which makes us
human.

Heal us
Remind us
Quicken us

Hold us
Whisper consolation
Amidst

37760907R00042

Made in the USA
Charleston, SC
15 January 2015